A l

...o Prayer

Meeting God where you are

by
Celia Wolf-Devine

All booklets are published thanks to the generous support of the members of the Catholic Truth Society

CATHOLIC TRUTH SOCIETY
PUBLISHERS TO THE HOLY SEE

Contents

An invitation to prayer

This booklet is an invitation to prayer, intended to help you start praying regularly or deepen your existing prayer life. Most people think of prayer as asking God for things for themselves or others, and regard it as what you do when things are really desperate. So far this is not wrong but prayer can be so much more. Regular prayer has always been regarded as an essential part of Christian life. In the psalms the believer is compared to a tree planted by a stream, that still bears fruit even in times of drought. They remain full of sap and green, even in old age. Jesus is the one who can give us living water, as he tells the Samaritan woman, [*Jn* 4:10] and prayer is an important way in which we can open ourselves to receive this so that we, too, can remain full of sap and green amid the trials of life.

As Christians we have a hope that non-Christians lack. We believe in a personal God who gives Himself to us in Christ and calls us to be with Him eternally. We seek to encounter this God in prayer, knowing that He is already seeking us. As Brother Lawrence put it "you need not cry very loud; he is closer to us than we are aware of"[1]. In prayer, then, we address ourselves to God. We direct our attention toward Him, invoke Him (calling upon His name), trying to open ourselves to Him and enter into a relationship with Him. It doesn't matter if our faith is a bit shaky; encountering God in prayer will strengthen it. For Jesus says "seek and you will find; knock and it will be opened to you." [*Lk* 11:9]

Christian meditation

Christians, then, engage in prayer with a certain background understanding of ourselves and God. The creeds set out clearly some of the core beliefs we share. We have the Scriptures as well as centuries of reflection and experience to draw upon to help us find our way. We understand the world through distinctively Christian categories. So while there is some overlap with spiritual practices engaged in by those involved with the "New Age" or by practitioners of Eastern religions, Christian prayer is not the same as any of these practices. Although the differences are sometimes subtle, they are nonetheless deep.

For example, Christians have long engaged in meditation – sometimes as a way to come to a deeper understanding of Sacred Scripture, or as a way to attain a quiet and receptive state while praying so that we can better listen to the Lord and allow Him to direct our prayer and our lives. We believe that when we set aside quiet time and try to turn within and listen to the Lord, we can discover His loving presence. St. Paul speaks of Christ dwelling in our hearts through faith. We want to find peace and joy through surrender and trust in God. We are in the image of God, and the Holy Spirit who dwells in us is God's free gift of grace through Jesus Christ.

Meditation in New Age circles is undertaken for different reasons – perhaps in order to help us learn to attain blissful states of consciousness or to have an experience in which the difference between oneself and ultimate reality is transcended. Many seek to attain mastery of their minds and bodily processes so that they can shape reality to be what they want it to be. Success, health and prosperity, they believe, can be ours if we learn to use our minds properly. A wide variety of things go under the umbrella term "New Age," so we need to be careful about generalizing, but many groups teach that there is a "God self" within us – that we are God and need only come to realize this. And although this sounds a bit like Christians turning within to listen to the Lord and finding Him present in their hearts, it is very different. On the Christian view, I do not create reality. Being made in the image of God our minds have creative powers, but we ourselves are created and sustained by Him at every moment, and our power is circumscribed by His.

Why pray?

Christians ought to pray for several reasons. In light of who God is and what He has done for us, it is right for us to give Him thanks and praise – to acknowledge Him humbly as our creator and worship Him with awe and reverence. We are encouraged in the Bible to "feel after Him and find Him," [*Acts* 17:27] to turn our hearts back to Him, to "behold the beauty of the Lord" [*Ps* 27:4] and worship in His temple. The Psalmist tells us to delight in the Lord and praise Him with song and musical instruments. He is holy and glorious and deserving of our love and worship even apart from what we ourselves may gain from prayer.

But worshiping Him also satisfies a deep need in us, by putting us in right relationship with the God who created and sustains us. No matter what we attain in a worldly way there is something in the human heart that remains dissatisfied and longs for more. We want to break free of the rat race, to breathe a freer air, to find a center of peace and strength and to experience a reality that grounds us and gives our lives meaning. The fact that you have picked up a book on prayer indicates that you have this sort of desire for something deeper, which means that God is already at work in you, drawing you to Him. This is comforting and encouraging in itself, for He will complete the good work He has begun in you. [*Phil* 1] Prayer offers God a space in which to work in our hearts and serves as a kind of golden thread that runs through our whole lives, until we attain to the satisfaction of our deepest desires in the Beatific Vision in Heaven.

And prayer also benefits others. I think of human beings as like corks connected to a net floating on the water. When one pulls down it pulls down the others, but especially those closest to it. When we let God lift us, it lifts others as well. We don't fully understand all the ways in which we are interconnected in the body of Christ, but in God's eyes we are. Prayer changes things. God uses our hearts to reinforce what He is doing in the hearts of others, especially those close to us. For there is a channel open from our heart to theirs and vice versa, so that God can work through us for each other when we pray.

Conversion of heart

Conversion of heart (also referred to as *metanoia*) is at the core of Christianity. The heart, as understood in the Bible, is not just the source of our emotions. It is the core or center of the whole person. As Christians we are becoming conformed to the image of Jesus Christ. St Paul speaks of us as coming to have the mind of Christ. We are not to be conformed to the world, but to be transformed by the renewal of our minds [*Rom* 12:2]. The sort of radical transformation we are called to is one that permeates all our faculties – not only our intellect and will, but also our imagination, emotions and desires. Our hearts must become like His heart. Faith can become dry and legalistic unless the deepest longings of our hearts become engaged, and prayer is the life blood of a faith that is vibrantly alive and growing.

Private and communal prayer

The Catholic tradition includes an extraordinarily rich variety of ways to pray, both communal and individual. The main focus of this booklet will be on private prayer, but private prayer and communal prayer are part of the same fabric. When we pray with others we are still alone with God in some sense, and when we pray by ourselves we are still with others. The reality of what is going on when we pray is deeper and richer than we realize.

Catholic churches always have pictures or statues of Mary and the saints. The Blessed Mother holds a special place in our devotions as she did in salvation history. Her presence is constantly there in the background, just as she was present in the gospels and in the early church, and we can always turn to her for help. We are "fellow citizens with the saints and members of the household of God." [*Eph* 2:19] There is a kind of intimacy and comfort here. The saints have finished their course, and we have not yet finished ours, but we are on the same road, and members of the same household. We can count on the prayers and companionship of Mary and the saints, and on the watchful care of God's holy angels.

The mass is the very heart of the Church's life and worship. This holy mystery lies at the root of who we are as Catholic Christians and permeates our devotional lives. It makes present once again Christ's passion and death and resurrection, and in participating in the mass we offer ourselves along with Jesus to the Father. In offering ourselves, and in turn being nourished with the Lord's own body and blood, we who are members of the mystical body of Christ are drawn more deeply into the life of God Himself. In the recitation of the Divine Office we join our prayers with the Church around the world to worship and praise God – a practice through which our understanding of our faith and love for Christ can become deeper. There are also many devotions to choose from such as the rosary, the chaplet of mercy, novenas or the stations of the cross, and these can be engaged in with others or by ourselves.

Communal prayer supports us when we are feeling a bit shaky in our faith. Worshiping side by side with so many people, (many of them strangers) can be uplifting. An old Protestant song says "There are many other Christians in the world today. I can feel the spirit moving when I hear them pray. And it gives me consolation when my soul is tried." Worshiping regularly with other Catholics and receiving the sacraments keeps us anchored in our tradition of faith and helps us grow in holiness, which enriches our private prayer life as well. But regular private prayer nourishes us and enables us to bring more to public worship – to participate more richly in it and get more out of it.

Getting past your blocks

If you find yourself always putting off prayer, and realizing at the end of the day that you haven't spent any time at all in prayer, you should think a little about what is holding you back. Prayer is a practice; there is no substitute for just sitting down and doing it. But knowing intellectually that prayer is good and that we should pray more doesn't always seem to be enough to motivate us to pray. There are different reasons for this, and one person's blocks may be different from another person's. But clearing away a few common reasons why people hold back from committing time to prayer may be helpful.

I'm too busy

If you are one of the many people who say "I really should try to pray regularly but I'm just too busy and stressed out to add one more thing to my life," you need to look at prayer differently. Don't think of it as another thing you have to *do*. Think of it more as a way to disengage yourself from the rush of practical activities and experience something of the leisureliness and eternity of God. Allow God to hold you and still you and work in you as He wills rather than trying to control everything. Even a short period of this sort of prayer is like finding an oasis in the desert. And after prayer you may find you can cross a lot of things off your list as worthless wastes of time, or that there is something you should do that hadn't occurred to you. You will feel less driven and more at peace. And there can be times in our lives when what God wants most from us *is* prayer.

Prayer is just a crutch for the weak

Another block can be the feeling that prayer is just for weak, pitiful people who need a crutch. We ought to be strong and handle things ourselves rather than bothering God. This sort of worry is completely wrong-headed for several reasons. First of all, lots of very strong people have prayed. Jesus Himself set us the example. And the time they spent with God in prayer was an important source of the heroic strength of the saints and martyrs down through the ages. What was available to saints in bygone ages is still available to us today; God hasn't changed, and human nature hasn't changed either. You may not be blessed with the constant sense of God's presence that Br. Lawrence was, or experience the sort of ecstatic states St. Theresa of Avila did, but don't rule out the possibility in advance. Countless people around us now are able to bear suffering and trials with courage and grace, and to accomplish extraordinary things because of the strength God gives them in prayer. Jesus wants us to experience joy and fulness of life, not just a sort of grim, stoical performance of our duty. God will lead us into the right path when we ask Him to, and show us ways in which we can use our talents creatively for good.

Second, the underlying myth that the strong person is the rugged individualist is just that – a myth. The person embedded in a supportive community is much better able to weather the storms of life than an isolated individual. And the one whose strength is grounded in his relationship with God is strongest of all. The Christian's motto might perhaps be "strength through dependence!" As an old Lutheran hymn put it: "on the rock of ages founded, what can shake thy sure repose?"

Speaking of prayer or religion in general as a crutch is common among atheists who think that they are superior because they have the courage to face the truth that there is no God. But if Christianity is true, then what could be more natural and appropriate than turning to our God in prayer and seeking His help and guidance? God is not "bothered" by our coming to Him. You can't put a gift into someone's hand if they hold their fist tightly clenched. Just so there are certain gifts God wants to give us that He can only give when we open our hands and hearts to receive them.

Bad experiences with Christians

If you have had bad experiences with Christians, especially those in positions of authority, this can sometimes interfere with prayer. If you find the face of someone who has hurt or betrayed you coming to mind when you are trying to pray, hold a crucifix or your favorite picture or icon of Jesus, and focus your attention on that. He, too, is grieved when those who profess to be Christians act in arrogant or destructive ways that wound or scandalize those who are genuinely seeking God. But remember there may be extenuating circumstances you don't know about. We should try to be merciful since we ourselves are in need of mercy. So say a quick prayer for that person if you can bring yourself to do it, and bring your focus back to the Lord.

Embarrassment

Sometimes we may hesitate to draw closer to God because we feel, in some vague sense, embarrassed. Embarrassment is a kind of primal self-protective impulse – an acute sense of being vulnerable and a fear of being open to the gaze of others. Being seen naked is a kind of paradigm case here. An adolescent who has a passionate crush on someone can be terrified of this being revealed to the object of his love or to others. People can be cruel; he may be rejected or laughed at. A woman may be terrified of letting anyone see her house when it is messy. Having a messy house is not sinful, yet people feel vulnerable. They wish everything was in order and beautiful, and don't want others to see the dirt and mess. In the same way, I think, we often feel afraid to invite God in. We want everything in us to be clean and orderly, but know that much is chaotic, conflicted, misshapen, even ugly.

The solution to this problem is two-fold. First, remember that God has befriended us in Christ. So just as you would go and visit someone out of friendship regardless of her messy house, so Jesus wants to come and be with us out of friendship. Second, only the action of the Holy Spirit can purify our hearts and set them in the right order. So if we wait until everything in us is orderly and beautiful before we let God in, we will wait forever. Fleeing God under these circumstances is like fleeing the doctor when we are sick.

I'm too sinful to pray

A more extreme sort of worry is the fear that God will not hear us because we are too sinful. You might think you have committed some sin that was so horrible that you cannot be forgiven. But God can forgive the worst of sinners. The only sin spoken of in the Bible as unforgivable is the sin against the Holy Spirit, but no one is very clear about just what that means, and you are very unlikely to have committed it. Consult a priest you respect if you are troubled by this sort of anxiety. Or your sense of being too sinful to pray may not stem from any particular sin you have committed, but from the feeling that for some unaccountable reason you are already lost or doomed. The temptation then is to give up hope and not even try to pray. But it is not all over until God says it is all over. God always gives us sufficient grace for salvation. Jesus died on the cross and rose again to free us from the power of sin and death, and you are always free to call upon Him to deliver you.

Fear that God will take you over

God never takes away our freedom; the Holy Spirit always guides us in ways that leave us free. If God wanted robots He would not have created us with free will. Love, to be love, must be freely given. His gift of Himself in Jesus Christ is His free gift to us. He wants us to accept that gift and respond by loving Him in return, and freely giving ourselves to Him. This level of intimacy and commitment, however, is something that we ordinarily grow into over a period of years, so don't feel you need to be able to just totally give yourself to God at the start. God understands our fears and our need to get to know Him gradually.

Not wanting to let go of things you are attached to

Don't let this sort of worry prevent you from stepping out into the path. God may, at some point, ask you to give up something you are attached to. But is this such a bad thing? Are we so sure that holding onto everything we are attached to will make us happy? Do we know what is for our real good? Might trying to gratify our every desire perhaps lead us to make a mess of our lives? Most of us have, I suspect, come up against the fact that doing everything our own way has not always made us happy. We need to seriously consider the possibility that God really does know us better than we know ourselves, and that if we enter into the walk with Him that He has planned for us, our lives will be fuller, richer, freer, more deeply satisfying than they would be if we let ourselves be blown about by our every whim and desire.

Be careful, however, not to second guess God about what He wants you to give up. You may suppose that of course God will want *you* to give up every earthly joy, attend only to solemn duties and serving the poor and prayer and fasting, and so on, and fear you are horribly worldly and selfish when you find yourself, quite naturally, shrinking back from this rather unattractive picture. Or you might justify your holding back from commitment to God by pointing to this model of Christian life. There are people called to ascetic lives, of course, but you may not be. Ask God to show you what He wants from you. He may want quite different sacrifices such as curbing your habits of complaining or running other people down, or insisting on controlling others and getting your own way. And even those called to lives of poverty and service to the poor like St. Francis did not go around being glumly dutiful, but radiated joy.

Fear that God wants you to give up what you most desire

A related, and quite common, fear is that God will ask us to give up what we most desire and therefore to sacrifice our happiness. In my experience, at least, what He wants of us first is to give up our desperate *attachment to* what we most desire – to stop making an idol of it. We keep thinking that if only we get this one thing we long for – a new dress or car, a husband, a good job, a baby – we will be satisfied, complete, happy. Of course we never are. That wonderful happiness we long for eludes us like a mirage as we approach it, and the longing attaches itself to something else. Advertisers stoke our desires to get us to buy their products, and our fevered attempt to get money to satisfy them crowds out our leisure, our time to enjoy nature or be with friends, time to do something significant to improve someone's life, and, of course, time for God.

St. Augustine said virtue is rightly ordered love and that our restless and insatiable desires cannot be satisfied in this world. Ultimately that deep yearning for completeness and fulfillment, he says, is a desire for God, and we cannot be happy until we find him. We should love God most because God is the highest and most perfect being, and then our neighbor for love of God. A harsh world-denying spirituality is not truly Christian. We are free to enjoy the world's good things and to love other people so long as we do not make idols of them by putting them before God.

God's grace alone can put our restless hearts in order and bring us peace, and prayer is one of the important ways in which God can work in us so that our desires become rightly ordered. Delight in the Lord and He will give you your heart's desire, says the psalmist. In the parable of the sower, Jesus speaks of the seed that fell among the thorns that grew up and choked it, comparing the thorns to the "cares of the world, and the delight in riches, and the desire for other things." [Mk 4:19] When we pray, God both satisfies and increases our desire for Him, so that the things we were so attached to no longer look so attractive to us by comparison with the joy we find in Him and giving them up is something we spontaneously want to do. If there is something you are doing that you have reason to believe is a sin, pray over a period of time asking God to show you the truth about it.

Some practical suggestions for prayer

You can address God in prayer any time. Through revelation and the Incarnation (the Word became flesh and dwelt among us *Jn* 1:14). God breaks into history from a place beyond the natural order of things. But He is also present at every point in the world, and thus we know that He is here with us now, so we can pray any time – while we are walking in the woods, or lying awake at night, alone or with people, in joy or sorrow, when beset by fear or pain, or when we feel thankful for some unexpected blessing. A moment of loving attention to Him, the repetition of His name, prayerfully singing a favorite hymn or song – all these are pleasing to Him and open us to receive His grace. But more extended periods of prayer provide an opportunity to deepen our relationship with God. Human friendship needs to be nurtured by spending time with one's friend, and our relationship with God does too. People are often very "religious" about exercising or watching their favorite TV show, and devotees of Eastern religions regularly commit a significant chunk of time to meditation. So set aside a block of time for God and be jealous for that time. Don't let other things begin to intrude on it and crowd it out.

In this chapter I will approach prayer by first discussing what I call "prayer of presence." This involves learning to simply sit in the presence of God with an attitude of openness and trust. I will next make some practical suggestions for setting up a regular prayer routine and dealing with some problems you may encounter. Finally, I will talk about a variety of ways in which prayer can begin to permeate the rest of your day in order to help you stay closer to the Lord, to become more attuned to what God wants of you, and to remain strong in the Lord in situations where others are indifferent or hostile to your faith.

Prayer of presence

It is one thing to believe through faith that God is present and another to experience His presence. We all want to have a vivid sense that God is really here with us. But don't assume that you are not experiencing God's presence if you do not feel something dramatic like St. Paul's encounter with Jesus on the road to Damascus. Our sense of His presence is often subtle and intermittent – a feeling that you are not alone, a heightened awareness of life, a moment of light and peace, a sense of being held and stilled, or comforted in times of sorrow and anguish, or perhaps a sudden clarity that reveals something deep about you and your situation.

Try closing your eyes and thinking of yourself as attempting to attune yourself to the thoughts and intentions of a person you know is in the room, but are unable to see (suppose it is dark). We can sometimes begin to do this with human beings, so try reaching out in the same way to the God who is so close to us, yet whom we cannot see. God's perception of us differs from the way other people perceive us because His perception extends to our inmost thoughts and desires – deeper by far than our own perception of ourselves. It would seem our perception of other people is much more reliable and clear than our perception of God, but the difference is less radical than it might seem. We can perceive only people's outer behaviors, and consequently may be badly mistaken about what is going on in them at a deeper level. And through the Incarnation, God reveals Himself to us in Jesus Christ, whose life provides a kind of body language, if you will, for understanding God and His intentions toward us. Finally, God may communicate with us directly as He did, for example, with St. Francis when he told him "rebuild my church." How this happens is mysterious, but that is to be expected.

Come as you are

Bring your *whole* self to God in prayer – not just your mind and will, but also your emotions, imagination, desires and body. Some people find physical gestures an aid to prayer. For example, you might feel moved to bow your head in worship, to hang your head in sorrow for your sins, to reach forward with your palms up in intercession, or to raise your hands high in praise. I find a seated position with my back and head comfortably supported works best for an extended period of prayer, but people differ about this sort of thing. If you are feeling upset, bring that to the Lord as well. The more you can bring to Him the more fully He can heal and transform you. Something in us desires God, and God knows how to find and fill that emptiness in us.

Be yourself

Often we have an image of what holy people should be like that can get in the way of our relationship with God. Some prayers are written in a very sweet and flowery style that may inspire one person and leave another cold. I think it is a good thing to use at least some set prayers, but choose ones you are comfortable with. Your set prayers provide a basic structure for your prayer time but allow time also for quiet reflection and for your own conversation with the Lord. No one else can write that script for you. Use whatever language comes naturally to you; God wants you to be the unique person He made you to be and not some sort of pasteboard image of what you think a saint should be like. The saints can be an inspiration for us, but don't try to imitate them slavishly. A saint is like a finger pointing to God. They became saints through the action of the Holy Spirit in them, so we too should invite that same spirit to work in us.

Depart from me for I am a sinful man

...when Simon Peter saw it [the miraculous catch of fish], he fell down at Jesus' knees, saying, "Depart from me, for I am a sinful man, O Lord." [Lk 5:8]

Any morally normal person is sometimes beset with feelings of guilt. And when you add to that the glory and holiness of God and the fact that He knows you fully as you are, sitting in His presence in an attitude of openness and trust may be difficult because we fear His judgment. But don't think of God as a harsh judge lying in wait to catch you in some sin. Yes, God sees our sins, but he also sees the goodness and uniqueness that he gave us, and our desire to follow his Son. He may see wonderful things in us that we don't even know are there. When we think of judgment, we think of one human being judging another, and this tends to be entangled with putting the other person down and all the nastiness that comes with our wounded and needy egos. God's judgment is clean; like light it reveals what is there. And in God's presence we can face the truth because His love is there sustaining us. That condemning edge that tempts us to despair is not of God.

Look at how Jesus Himself behaved. People were very shocked by the way he treated sinners. The Pharisees would have shunned such people. They complained that "this man welcomes sinners and eats with them." [*Lk* 15:2 Jerusalem Bible] Table fellowship was, in the ancient world, a special sacred bond, and Jesus' willingness to extend this to tax collectors and prostitutes was a clear indication of how widely God's invitation extends. "I came not to call the righteous, but sinners." [*Mat* 9:13] And as St. Paul puts it: "while we were yet sinners, Christ died for us." [*Rom* 5:8]

Getting a prayer routine in place

We are creatures of habit. Prayer should become part of
your everyday routine. It helps, I think, if you can develop
a little ritual around your prayer time, because it becomes
a habit more easily. Try to pray regularly at roughly the
same time each day. Choose a private place, if possible.
Having a regular prayer space can help, but if you travel a
lot you can still maintain your regular prayer routine. Just
arrange the pillows against the wall or headboard of your
bed so that your back is comfortable and pray as usual.

I will begin by sharing my own prayer routine because
I think it is helpful to have something concrete to work
from for a start. I encourage you to give it a try and take
from it what you find useful. Over time you will find what
works best for you. I pray first thing in the morning. The
basic structure I use is as follows. Firstly I begin by easing
into prayer, then I say a few opening prayers, this is
followed by an invocation of Holy Spirit, then a surrender
prayer, and finally an appeal to the Heart of Jesus.

Pray slowly and reflectively, attending to the meaning
of the words but not getting into analyzing them too much.
Words are like ships moving over the face of the water;
much moves with them under the surface that we do not
see. The words we pray give God a chance to work in us at

deep levels; He can write on our souls through them so we become more strongly formed in our faith and conformed to the image of Christ. Don't feel you have to finish the prayers. If you feel the Lord's presence for a moment, pause and rest in Him rather than just slogging on saying the prayers. I think it is good to memorize as much of your regular prayers as you can so you can say them with your eyes closed and use them freely in any situation.

You may not have time for really extended prayer in the morning, but you should try to begin your day with at least a little prayer. The Christian tradition has always seen the morning as an especially privileged time for prayer. Go to bed earlier to make time for it. Don't worry if you are not at your peak of mental alertness. Come to Him in all your morning fogginess and let Him draw you out and prepare you for the day. People with small children may have a hard time with prayer in the morning, and it helps if you have someone to run interference for you. But as soon as they are old enough to understand, it is good for them to learn that prayer is an important activity that is part of normal adult life. "Don't bother Mummy when she is sitting in her prayer chair" is something they can be taught to respect. But if you find praying in the morning just won't work for you then adapt what I say for use at whatever time you choose to pray.

Easing into prayer

If, like me, you need a little caffeine to get going, get up and make your coffee or tea. Then sit down right away to pray. I sip my tea as I start to pray, and find that having something warm, sweet and comforting to drink eases the transition into prayer. I begin by reading the scripture lessons from the day's Mass. Read slowly and reflectively. Then bring to the Lord things that are on your mind and let them go. Perhaps something you feel bad about from yesterday can be brought to Him for forgiveness and let go of. Try to set aside any feelings of anger or resentment you might have, asking God's help to do so. Perhaps you have some special intention, or there may be a person you care about in special need that you want to lift up to the Lord. Or you may need guidance about what to do in some situation. Hand these things over to God and let them go.

A small ritual, rich with meaning, is making the sign of the cross. I hold my hand in the way the Orthodox do. Place your little finger and ring finger flat against your palm, and hold the thumb and other fingers together, saying "*two natures in one person, Jesus Christ, true God and true man; three persons in one God. I pray in the name of the Father, the Son, and the Holy Spirit.*" This makes clear who we are invoking, and puts the central tenets of our faith front and center.

Opening prayers

God come to my assistance; Lord make haste to help me. Glory be to the Father and to the Son and to the Holy Spirit as it was in the beginning, is now and will be forever. (This is used at the start of all the hours of prayer in the Divine Office).

Almighty God unto whom all hearts are open, all desires known, and from whom no secrets are hid, cleanse the thoughts of our hearts by the inspiration of thy holy spirit that we may perfectly love thee and worthily magnify thy holy name. (From the *Book of Common Prayer*)

Holy Spirit invocation hymn

Jesus tells the Samaritan woman that true worshipers will worship the Father "in spirit and truth." We pray to the Father, in the Spirit and through the Son. The Holy Spirit helps us pray, so it is good to invoke Him whenever we sit down to pray and ask Him to come dwell in us and make us new. There are a number of hymns, sequences or songs invoking the Holy Spirit that you might wish to use. This is the one I use.

Come Creator, Spirit come, and make within our souls Thy home. Supply Thy grace and heavenly aid to fill the Hearts which Thou hast made.

Oh gift of God most high, Thy name is Comforter whom we acclaim the fount of life and fire of love and sweet anointing from above.

The sevenfold gift of grace is thine, Thou finger of the hand divine. The Father's promise true to teach our earthly tongues Thy heavenly speech.

Thy light to every sense impart, pour forth thy grace in every heart. Our weakened flesh do thou restore to strength and courage evermore.

Oh most blessed light divine, shine within these hearts of thine, and our inmost being fill. Where thou art not man hath nought, nothing good in deed or thought, nothing free from taint of ill.

Heal our wounds, our strength renew, on our dryness pour thy dew; wipe the stains of guilt away.

Bend the stubborn heart and will, melt the frozen, warm the chill, guide the steps that go astray.

On the faithful who adore and confess thee evermore, in thy sevenfold gift descend.

Drive far away our spirit's foe, thine own abiding peace bestow. Where thou dost go before as guide, no evil can our steps betide.

Through thee may we the Father learn, and know the Son and Thee discern, who art of both and thus adore perfectly for evermore.

Amen.

Surrender prayer

This prayer is good because it does not limit what God may do in us, but doesn't require us to give everything over to God all at once.

Heavenly Father, please help me to surrender to you now and all day more than yesterday. Help me receive you and allow you to dwell in me more deeply than yesterday and to live in you and for you more today than yesterday.

Appeal to the Heart of Jesus

It is in the heart of Jesus Christ that divinity and humanity touch and intermingle most intimately. So God can now touch our hearts through a human heart like our own. The pierced heart has long been a symbol of love. Cupid carries a bow and arrows with which he pierces the lover's heart, and Valentines show a heart with an arrow through it. Jesus' heart was pierced upon the cross, and from it flowed blood and water – that living water for which we thirst. And in the Eucharist we receive that mingled water and blood when we receive the cup. Through His heart the transforming power of God's love is poured into our hearts.

The Litany of the Sacred Heart

I pray at least part of the Litany of the Sacred Heart each day and recommend this practice.

Lord have mercy;
Christ have mercy;
Lord have mercy;
Christ hear us.
Christ graciously hear us.
God the Father of Heaven, (have mercy on us);
(Repeat this response after each invocation)
God the Son, Redeemer of the world,
God the Holy Spirit, Sanctifier of the faithful,
Holy Trinity, one God,
Heart of Jesus, Son of the Eternal Father,
Heart of Jesus, Formed by the Holy Spirit in the womb of the virgin mother,
Heart of Jesus, substantially united to the Word of God,
Heart of Jesus, of infinite majesty,
Heart of Jesus, sacred temple of God,
Heart of Jesus, tabernacle of the Most High,
Heart of Jesus, house of God and gate of Heaven,
Heart of Jesus, burning furnace of charity,
Heart of Jesus, abode of justice and love,
Heart of Jesus, full of goodness and love,
Heart of Jesus, abyss of all virtues,
Heart of Jesus, most worthy of all praise,

Heart of Jesus, king and center of all hearts,
Heart of Jesus, in whom are all the treasures of
wisdom and knowledge;
Heart of Jesus, in whom dwells all the fulness
of divinity,
Heart of Jesus, in whom the Father is well pleased,
Heart of Jesus, of whose fulness we have all received,
Heart of Jesus, desire of the everlasting hills,
Heart of Jesus, patient and most merciful,
Heart of Jesus, enriching all who invoke you,
Heart of Jesus, fountain of life and holiness,
Heart of Jesus, propitiation for our sins,
Heart of Jesus, loaded down with opprobrium,
Heart of Jesus, bruised for our offenses;
Heart of Jesus, obedient to death,
Heart of Jesus, pierced with a lance; source of
all consolation,
Heart of Jesus, our life and resurrection,
Heart of Jesus, our peace and reconciliation
Heart of Jesus, victim for our sins,
Heart of Jesus, salvation of those who hope in you,
Heart of Jesus, hope of those who die in you,
Heart of Jesus, delight of all the saints.

The final prayers are:

Lamb of God, you take away the sins of the world,
spare us O Lord.
Lamb of God, you take away the sins of the world,
graciously hear us O Lord.
Lamb of God, you take away the sins of the world, have
mercy on us.
Jesus meek and humble of heart, make our hearts like
to yours.

Almighty and eternal God, look upon the heart of your
dearly beloved Son our Lord Jesus Christ and on the
praises and satisfaction he offers you in the name of
sinners, and to those who implore your mercy, of your
great goodness grant forgiveness. Through the same
Christ our Lord.

Amen.

Background images for prayer
that you may find helpful

The way we think about ourselves in relation to God structures our response to Him. Imaginative images help us grasp unseen realities. Jesus, himself, used analogies of this sort constantly. He speaks of vineyards, wine skins, mustard seeds, yeast, pearls, sheep and shepherds, and of course the extended analogies we call parables – the prodigal son for example. How do we think of ourselves in relation to God? God as a loving Father has a certain primacy for Christians, since Jesus Himself taught us to call Him "Father." But there are many other images we can use when praying that will facilitate an attitude of receptivity and trust. One that is firmly grounded in Scripture is the parable of the sower. We have received the Word. St. James says: "receive with meekness the implanted Word which is able to save your souls" [*Jas* 1:21]. Will we allow it to take root in us deeply – holding it fast in a generous and faithful heart so that it can bear much fruit – or will it be eaten by birds or choked out by weeds. Ask God in prayer to root out some of the weeds and soften the dry, hard ground of our hearts with life-giving rain.

An image, common in the mystical literature, is thinking of God shaping and molding us as a potter shapes the clay, or a sculptor a piece of marble. The image of the soul as a house or dwelling which we invite God to enter is also a common one. Thinking of God as breathing His Spirit into us is a wonderful image as well. As God breathed the spirit first into Adam so that he became a living being, so through Christ a new supernatural life is breathed into us. Sometimes we may feel assaulted and invaded like a city under siege and think of Jesus as a warrior and victorious king coming to deliver us from all evil and darkness. "May the light of Christ rising in glory dispel the darkness of our hearts and minds." (Easter vigil prayer)

Many mystics have described their experience of God as like that of an infant nursing at the breast. They usually use this maternal imagery of God longing to nourish us with His life quite comfortably without changing the pronouns used for God. Drinking from a spring so that we are filled and satisfied is another useful image. "Oh God, thou art my God, I seek thee, my flesh faints for thee as in a dry and weary land where no water is." [Ps 63:1] Bridal imagery has also been common among some mystics. Such mystics (male and female) think of Jesus as the bridegroom of their souls. The imagery used is drawn in part from the Song of Songs, so if you feel drawn to this way of thinking about your relationship with Jesus, you might open your Bible to that and pray those parts of it that you are attracted to.

The Lord may inspire you with a special way He wants you to think about your relationship to Him and what He wants from you, so be open to that. A few images I have found helpful are: Thinking of myself as a drowning swimmer and Jesus as the lifeguard coming to rescue me. This reminds me to stop thrashing around and relax so He can get a hold of me and draw me out of the deep waters.

You might try thinking of Jesus as a partner leading you in a dance. You need to be as responsive as possible to His least pressure so that you can move as one. If two people dance together often this sort of attunement gets better so that you can respond at once to your partner's lead, and over time we should learn to follow Jesus more and more closely without His having to shove or correct us all the time.

Thinking of God as a life-giving source of light and warmth like the sun can help engender an attitude of trust and receptivity. Imagine yourself sunbathing, letting God warm and soften you. Or think of yourself, perhaps, as a flower that turns toward the light and opens its petals to give off its sweetness.

A few common problems in prayer

Distractions

Virtually everyone is sometimes beset with distractions when praying. When your mind wanders, just bring it back to the prayers. If you don't remember where you were, start anywhere. It is our desire to worship God and enter into relationship with Him that matters, and not our recitation of particular prayers in the correct order. Do not get upset at yourself over your poor concentration. Prayer is more something God does in us than something we do. It might help to keep a pad of paper next to you and if something really important occurs to you that you need to do and are afraid of forgetting, jot it down and return to prayer.

Scruples

People with high spiritual aspirations frequently suffer from scrupulosity. They worry that their prayer won't work, or that God won't hear them because they aren't doing it right, or because they don't have the proper motivation. Such people tend to pick at themselves and find fault with themselves a lot. Don't expect perfection of yourself and try to keep your focus on God rather than on monitoring yourself. Of course we are imperfect and our motives are mixed; that's why we need God. Don't worry whether you have the right feelings. Prayer is not just a statement of your current feelings, but an expression of your intentions to worship, praise and thank God, to come to know and love and serve Him better and to become the person He created you to be.

Discouragement

Don't become discouraged if you don't feel like anything is happening when you pray, for God can work in us on all sorts of levels and in ways we do not understand. Prayer will bear fruit in your life, but don't expect God to transform you instantaneously. Bad patterns in our lives have developed over many years, and usually don't disappear immediately. The fruits of the spirit are love, joy, peace, patience, kindness, goodness, faithfulness, gentleness and self control [*Gal* 5:22-23]. In prayer we invite the Holy Spirit to come and dwell in us. So over an extended period of time, you will, hopefully, begin to notice some improvements – more patience, less attraction to some of your besetting sins, a stronger faith and a more charitable attitude toward others, for example. Sometimes God might heal you of a problem you didn't even know you had. Suddenly one day you notice that something has changed. But remember God is the judge; we are not. He will bring to completion the good work He has begun in us in His own way and in His own time. And as your faith life deepens over time you will become more able to recognize His presence with you, both in prayer and as you go about the rest of your life.

Temptations

Temptations of many sorts may beset you during prayer. We can get obsessed by desires that pull us toward doing something we know we should not do. If this happens to you confess your powerlessness, beg God to help you and try to turn your attention to something else. We are drawn towards what we focus our attention on, which is why the saints advise us to direct our attention to God as much as we can. We can also be tempted to succumb to sloth, laziness, or despair which lead us to give up our devotional practices and put off doing good deeds. Remember, though, if you don't keep moving forward you will slip back.

On the most general level, the big temptation is simply the desire to have one's own will rather than to serve God. The Devil's motto is *non serviam* (I will not serve). Sometimes this desire can sweep through you powerfully like an inner runaway horse almost in spite of yourself. I think this sort of temptation occurs when God is calling us into a deeper relationship with Him, so take advantage of this to say "yes" to God and move forward to a new level of life with Him. Don't be upset if you experience this sort of temptation; there is something in all of us that stands against God. Sometimes when beset by powerful temptations it is helpful to realize that it is not all just you. The Holy Spirit breathes life into our good impulses, and negative spirits try to inflame our bad ones to get us to turn away from God. How much is from ourselves and how much might be the result of the action of negative spirits is in practice difficult to determine, and there is no need to try. Only the God who created us can understand our hearts in all their murky depths and only He can heal them. So resist the temptation to give up in despair when your weaknesses overwhelm you and you get a glimpse for a moment of how deeply willfulness, selfishness and sin pervade your heart. For however wide and deep the corruption of our hearts, God's mercy extends just as widely. And this is cause for rejoicing. So turn to God with your whole heart in times of temptation.

Doubts

Although you may experience the presence of God in prayer on some occasions, it is easy afterwards to start worrying about whether you really did. Perhaps it was just your imagination. If people close to you are anti-religious or have a kind of blank incomprehension of what it is all about, you may slip into seeing things through their eyes and start to lose confidence in your own lived experience. Don't let this happen. Hold on to it and treasure it. There is a part in each of us that is for God alone so don't allow other people's judgments to invade that space, especially those of people hostile to religion. If they chose to turn away from God that is their business, but you be faithful to your call. If you need advice go to a more mature Christian to help you, but even then don't pour out everything right away.

Religious pluralism can also engender doubts in us. Don't we just find the Christian God because that is what we are expecting to find? Moslems or Buddhists have religious experiences as well that seem to confirm their beliefs. Why take ours to reveal the truth? We can only start from where we are. The Christian tradition has a rich and complex understanding of God and provides a well trodden path in the wilderness through which we may approach Him and grow into an ever-deepening communion of knowledge and love with the God who created, redeemed and sustains us. Saints and ordinary believers throughout the ages testify to the riches God has poured out on those who seek him with all their hearts. So we have good reason to set out on the path we have been given without having to investigate every other path and be sure that none of them leads there as well. In fact, if one looks at the variety of world religions, it becomes clear that they do not all understand the goal of the spiritual path in the same way, but to show this would require another book.

Prayer throughout the day

It is wonderful to have a daily routine that makes time for prayer and to find fruitful ways of praying during those times. But what about all the other times? Our Catholic faith should pervade our lives at every level. This can be difficult under the best of circumstances, and being surrounded by a highly secular culture makes it even harder. When swimming against the stream in this sort of way it is hard to resist the temptation to go native and conform to the values of those around us, or at least to compartmentalize our lives so that our Sunday self doesn't connect with what we do and think the rest of the week. Prayer can help. Some of the types of prayer described below can be done as background to your other activities; others take longer or require going to a special place. See what you feel drawn to.

Prayer at set hours

One thing you can do is to say short prayers at set times during the day just to bring yourself back to God for a moment. If you have time, of course, doing the Divine Office at the various hours of prayer is an excellent practice[2]. But a few short prayers can also help. The Angelus is commonly said at noon, many people say a quick prayer at 3 p.m. (the hour Jesus died on the cross). A little prayer as day fades into night (evening prayer) bringing your day to God and asking His blessing on your evening gives you time to collect yourself at the end of the day. If you can stop by a church on your way home from work for five minutes of prayer it can make a lot of difference in your evening. It is always good to pray in front of the Blessed Sacrament if you can. And be sure to say a little prayer before sleep – minimally an Our Father. Bedtime can also be a good time for thanking God for whatever blessings you have received that day.

Our day does not end when we get in bed; many hours of darkness lie between bedtime and dawn. One of the regular monastic hours of prayer is vigils, which is done in the middle of the night. Busy lay people with jobs and family may not want to make this part of their regular routine, but some people find this an especially wonderful time to pray. A deep stillness settles over the world while everyone is asleep and this lends a special feeling of intimacy to time spent alone with God then. Night is also a time when we can feel especially vulnerable when unable to sleep. Our bodily energy hits its lowest point during the night, which allows physical and emotional pains to surface more strongly. Tasks we need to do run through our minds. Fears and worries assault us. Prayer can help. It is a good idea to actually get up to pray because this helps us break free of the thought patterns we are caught in and feel less helpless. Praise Him, ask for His protection, talk to Him from your heart, and hand everything over to Him.

Prepare with prayer

Prayer can smooth our way throughout the day and open us to God's guidance. Always say a quick prayer before you enter into a situation that is new or difficult. Prayer should be your first resort, not your last resort. And give thanks for the good things – deliverance from danger, moments of warm fellowship, something beautiful or touching that you see. Use time that would otherwise be wasted to pray. For example while waiting in a line or driving your car. Cars are a wonderful place to pray in complete privacy – to say a few memorized prayers or to pour out your heart to God.

Calling on the name of Jesus

Saint Paul advises us to pray constantly, and one way to do this is the Jesus prayer. The full prayer is "Jesus Christ, Son of God, have mercy on me a sinner." Some coordinate this prayer with their breathing, breathing in on the first half and out on the second. Shorter forms are "Jesus, mercy!" or just "Jesus." To speak someone's name is to invoke, call or summon them. And the name of Jesus is not just like any other name. It has power. In Acts a cripple is healed by the name of Jesus [*Acts* 4:7-12], and demons cast out in his name, even by people who were disciples [*Mk* 9:38]. A man I know was in a terrible car accident and just went limp and called out "Jesus." He emerged unhurt although the police were surprised he had survived at all. You can also pray "please Jesus" (He knows what we need better than we do) or "Jesus, yes" (expressing willingness to be led by Him).

Try repeating His name in your mind when you are in a very delicate situation – say, for example, someone is opening up to you about something very personal and painful. It keeps you from jumping in too soon in a heavy handed way and invites Jesus to work in both of you for good. Or when you are feeling especially beset by fear or doubt. Pray "Jesus I love you" frequently, especially when you have just a little glimmer of feeling His presence. This is not just a description of what you are feeling, but an expression of your desire to love Him and a prayer for Him to give you the love to love Him and draw you into union with Him.

Intercession

We should pray regularly for those close to us, for those in positions of civil and religious authority, and for Christians everywhere (especially those suffering persecution). Pray that God will bless and help whoever is sick or injured when you see an ambulance go by, or for people you pass in the street who look sad. And pray, of course, for causes and concerns especially close to your own heart. It is usually a good idea not to be too specific about what we are asking God to do, but rather to just bring the problem to Him and let Him resolve it. It helps if you can find a few friends who you feel comfortable asking for prayers. And don't neglect to ask Mary and the saints to intercede for you as well. Jesus on the cross gave the church Mary to be our mother, and remembering her role in Jesus' first miracle at the wedding at Cana, we can trust in the efficacy of her intercession with her son.

Praying with Scripture (lectio divina)

Doing at least some prayerful reading of Scripture would be a good thing to fit into your daily routine. Choosing the Mass readings for the day is a good idea because they are chosen specifically for worship. Pray that the Holy Spirit will help you understand more deeply, reflect on each phrase slowly, see what God seems to be communicating to you personally through this scripture, and see if you feel that the Lord is moving you to do something to put into practice what you have learned. Scripture is inspired by God, and prayerful reflection on it nourishes our faith and guides us in our lives.

The Stations of the Cross

This devotion is one that many people find moving and comforting. Every Catholic church has some sort of artistic representation of the stations of the cross. These make vivid what Jesus suffered for us, and can help us to enter more deeply into the Passion of Our Lord. What He suffered shows us the depth of His love for us, and we can bring our own sufferings to Him so He can help us bear them by taking them up into His own. You can use a booklet with set prayers for each station. Or you can just walk around looking at each one in turn, trying to imaginatively enter into it and say a little prayer of your own.

Adoration of the Blessed Sacrament

From the earliest days, the Church would set aside the Eucharist for the sick who could not attend Mass. Since Jesus Christ is truly present in the Eucharist under the form of bread and wine, Christians gradually started to spend time praying in the presence of the Blessed Sacrament. Today, Catholic churches keep the Sacrament reserved in a locked tabernacle as our most precious treasure, with a sanctuary light constantly burning next to it, and the Church strongly encourages us to spend time adoring the Blessed Sacrament. Although God is present everywhere, he is present in the Blessed Sacrament in a unique way, and as countless Christians can verify from their own experience, being close to the Blessed Sacrament brings special graces in prayer. You can just walk into a church and pray near the tabernacle by yourself. Many parishes also have regular times of exposition, where the Blessed Sacrament is displayed in a monstrance so we can gaze upon it. This is sometimes followed by benediction which contains a few beautiful prayers and ends with the priest bestowing a special blessing with the monstrance.

The Rosary

This widely beloved prayer is one that fits well with contemplative prayer, though it may also be used for intercession without prolonged meditation on the mysteries. When using it to meditate on the mysteries, your mind works on several levels. You say the words, but at the same time reflect on various important events in salvation history. You can use a scriptural rosary booklet and think about a different scripture passage for each bead. Or you can try to enter into and visualize or imagine each scene. You can think of yourself as praying with Mary seeing things through her eyes, as it were – asking her to help you grow closer to her son as you pray. Or just place yourself in the presence of God and direct your attention to Him as you pray.

The Litany of the Sacred Heart

You can also use the Litany of the Sacred Heart for meditation or for intercession. When using it for intercession I sometimes think of myself crying out to

Him each time I say "Lord have mercy" as though shooting an arrow upward. Other times I think of myself as a baby bird, naked, featherless, helpless and huddled down in the nest. The little birds are afraid to make any noise lest it attract predators, and can only trust that their parents will return and feed them. Just so we must trust the Lord to be faithful and not forget us. We can't find Him but He can always find us.

Praying in tongues

Charismatic prayer is something many people shy away from; images of people babbling weirdly and falling into fits come to mind. The practice is well grounded in Christian tradition, however, and can be done in a quiet and reverent way. Some Catholic churches have Life in the Spirit seminars at the end of which you can get prayed over to receive the Holy Spirit, though you can also receive this gift while praying alone. Think of yourself as praising Him along with the angels and saints, and ask Him for a tongue to praise Him. The Holy Spirit prays in us and through us, and if you feel praise welling up and flowing out in this way just allow it to flow. This can afford a wonderful sense of intimacy with God and a delight in praising him. It can strengthen our faith when we feel shaky or serve as a way to intercede for others.

Prayer in times of desolation

Out of the depths I cry to thee, O Lord [*Ps* 130]: Although we keep up appearances for others, our hearts are sometimes beset by fear and loneliness and feelings of desolation can flood in upon us. If you experience these don't feel there is something terribly wrong with you. An overly sunny view of what Christians should be like can be a real stumbling block for those who are going through grief and loss, severe illness or unrelenting pain, despair over their own weakness, sinfulness, or hardness of heart, humiliation, failure, betrayal by someone they trusted, and who are feeling abandoned by God. Many saints have struggled with despair, including St. Therese of Lisieux (the "Little Flower") who is often thought of as a sweet, simple, sunny person. The Psalms can be a wonderful resource for us when going through such experiences because they include the full range of human emotion and we can use them to pour out our hearts to God when we are in deep distress. Jesus, on the cross, prayed *Psalm* 22. *Psalm* 88, which concludes "My one companion is darkness," expresses profound desolation and is recited during night prayer each Friday as part of the Divine Office.

The psalms, although they express so many varieties of anguish and desolation are remarkable because often even in the same psalm we suddenly find verses of lyrical beauty praising and glorifying God. Psalm 42 for example says "My soul is cast down within me, therefore I remember thee... Deep calls to deep at the thunder of thy cataracts; all thy waves and thy billows have gone over me..." ends with "Hope in God; for I shall again praise him, my help and my God." Even Psalm 22 has verses like "The afflicted shall eat and be satisfied; those who seek him shall praise the Lord." Remembering to praise God even in the midst of suffering can open us to God's grace and peace.

The important thing is to remember that whatever you are going through God is there with you, and that Jesus Himself suffered pain, humiliation and betrayal. He sweated blood in the garden of Gethsemane. He makes our burdens His own and helps us bear them. This may not make the suffering go away, but in Him it becomes bearable; strength is given to us and a little point of peace in which our soul can rest and be upheld by Him, even when all around is at its darkest. Jazz musician Tommy Dorsey's song/prayer written after the death of his wife and baby provides us a good model for prayer at such times. "Precious Lord, take my hand. Lead me on, let me stand! I am tired, I am weak, I am worn. Through the storm, through the night, lead me on to the light. Take my hand precious Lord, lead me home."

It can be discouraging if you, at one time, did feel the Lord's presence and love, and now He seems to be absent. Of course this does not mean that He really is absent; "Lo I am with you always even to the end of the age." [*Mt* 28:20] There can be any number of reasons why we might stop feeling God's presence that don't imply that we are doing anything wrong. We notice a change more than a static state. So when we are going through a deep change like a conversion experience, we feel the movement of the Spirit strongly, but when the Spirit has settled in we may notice Him less and take Him for granted, forgetting what our inner life was like before. Spiritual life has its own rhythms and cycles and you may well come to experience Him strongly again. And sometimes the Spirit may be poured out especially on us for some particular mission or trial we are to meet that day. Different cases vary, so ask God to show you what is going on.

The really tough case is when you have become used to a sense of intimacy with the Lord, and slowly or suddenly this disappears and this emptiness continues for a long time. Mother Teresa of Calcutta suffered in this way for many years. Yet, in spite of her inner darkness, her smile lit up the room and she brought God's love to millions. Perhaps feeling herself rejected and abandoned by God gave her special graces to minister to the needs of those she served who were themselves rejected and abandoned. But God's purposes ultimately remain opaque and any neat answers fall short of the mystery of suffering. An old American hymn portrays a person experiencing this dreadful trial. After having had wonderful experiences of God's love, the speaker says: "my complaint is bitter now, for all my joys are gone; I've strayed! I'm left! I know not how; the light's from me withdrawn... What shall I do? Shall I lie down and sink in deep despair? Will He forever wear a frown, nor hear my feeble prayer? No; He will put His strength in me, He knows the way I've strolled, and when I'm tried sufficiently I shall come forth as gold[3]."

Towards singleness of heart

The heart is the core or center of the person. An old Sacred Harp song enjoins us to "serve with a single heart and eye; and to thy [Jesus'] glory live or die[4]." To have integrity we must be the same person in every context. Yes, the way we express ourselves will differ depending on who we are with, but our heart should not waver or become divided. Our relationship with God should overflow into all our human relationships. As we have received, so we must also give. Anger, hardness of heart and unwillingness to forgive are some of the important ways in which we often block the flow of God's love from us to others. Forgiveness is not optional for Christians. It is right there in the Lord's prayer. So ask God to help you forgive. Remember the story about the servant who had been forgiven a huge debt and then went out and refused the plea of a fellow servant who owed him a mere fraction of that amount, and how harsh that servant's punishment was.

There are things that should make us angry in the world. But don't let the anger eat you up. Do whatever you can to alleviate the situation and turn your mind to something else. Nursing anger can poison us on all sorts of levels, incapacitate us for enjoying life and doing the good we are here to do, and make us into the sort of person people flee from. St. Paul says "If you are angry, let it be without sin. The sun must not go down on your wrath; do not give the devil a chance to work on you." [*Eph* 4:26-27]. Never pass final judgment on anyone, including yourself. One of the wonderfully freeing things about Christianity is the truth that God alone is the judge of the human heart. What a burden off us! A person's actions may be objectively sinful, and making a judgment about this is appropriate. But we can never know all the possible mitigating factors and judge the intentions of their heart. If you struggle with a tendency to judge others harshly, pray that God will help you see them as He sees them. This can yield surprising results sometimes.

If Jesus is the center – the anchor – then we should make all our choices mindfully, evaluating them in terms of how they impact our relationship with God. What kind of work do we do? Who do we spend time with? What do we do for fun? Who do we go to for help when we feel like we just can't cope? What movies or TV programs do we watch? What books do we read? The imagination is important for prayer and provides a kind of background climate to our minds, so the images we stock it with affect us. People differ widely in their sensitivities, so you need to evaluate things as they impact you. I'm not recommending reading or watching nothing but pious schlock. But be mindful of what you are taking in.

The hope to which we are called

The underlying theme of this booklet has been the way in which prayer can give God the space to work in us and transform our hearts to make them more like the heart of His son Jesus. Our heart's desire for God can only be fully satisfied after this life when we are united with Him eternally. Union with God is not a matter of losing ourselves in Him as a drop of water blends into the sea; it is a matter of simultaneous giving and receiving. We give ourselves to God and He gives Himself to us. He receives our gift of ourselves and we receive Him. God is an inexhaustible source of love and life; hence our desire for Him must be capable of endless growth. In Heaven, I believe, we will not experience Him all at once, but rather be drawn deeper and deeper into His love. God will endlessly satisfy our desire for Him and call us to new and deeper levels of desire and enjoyment of His being and His love. We will grow then into a deeper union with God without limit and without end. This, then, is the desire of our hearts, and the hope to which we are called.

Acknowledgements

I am grateful to Stratford Caldecott for his helpful suggestions, to Fr. Nicholas Lombardo, O.P. for his careful and insightful reading of the manuscript and his constructive ideas for improving it, to Edith Black for help with my discussion of the Eucharist, to my husband Phil Devine for help clarifying and polishing passages I was struggling with, and to all those whose prayers have sustained me on the way.

Further reading

CTS Deeper Christianity series. The fourth Part of the Catechism of the Catholic Church is on prayer.

Brother Lawrence of the Resurrection. *The Practice of the Presence of God.* Critical Edition by Donald Attwater (NewYork Phoenix Press, 1985)

Foley, Marc, OCD. *The Love that Keeps us Sane: Living the Little Way of St. Therese of Lisieux* (Mahwah N.J.: Paulist Press, 2000)

Foster, Richard. *Prayer: Finding the Heart's True Home* (New York, HarperCollins Publishers, 1992) (A Christian theologian in the Quaker tradition)

Dr Gray, Tim *Praying Scripture for a Change: An Introduction to Lectio Divina* (West Chester, PA: Ascension Press, 2009

Groeschel, Benedict CFR (ed). *Praying in the Presence of our Lord: Prayers for Eucharistic Adoration* (Huntington IN: Our Sunday Visitor, 1999)

Hume, Cardinal Basil. *A Spiritual Companion.* (Brewster, Mass.: Paraclete Press, 2001). First published in London by Darton, Longman and Todd

Sri, Edward. *The New Rosary in Scripture* (Cincinnati, OH: St. Anthony Messenger Press, 2003)

Wolf-Devine, Celia. *The Heart Transformed: Prayer of Desire* (N.Y.: Alba House/Society of St. Paul, 2009)

Amy Welborn. *The Words we Pray: Discovering the Richness of the Catholic Tradition* (Chicago: Loyola Press, 2005)

Endnotes

[1] *Brother Lawrence of the Practice of the Presence of God*, p. 68

[2] *Christian Prayer* available from Catholic Book Publishing Corp. is the official one volume edition of the Liturgy of the Hours (Divine Office).

[3] *The Sacred Harp*, 1991 edition. (Sacred Harp Publishing Company, p. 67)

[4] *The Sacred Harp*, (p. 448)

Scripture quotations are taken from the RSV.

Handbook of Novenas
to the Saints

A novena is a way of praying, often for a particular intention or need. It consists, very simply, of a prayer or prayers said for nine (usually consecutive) days. This booklet contains newly composed novena prayers asking for the intercession of various saints. The long experience of praying Christians, and the teaching of the Church, assure us that the duty of Christians to support each other with prayer does not end with this life, and the saints delight to add their voices to ours when we make our requests to God our Father.

Each novena is prefaced with a short biography of the saint, which gives some suggestions of the particular intentions or needs where their intercession has been found especially powerful.

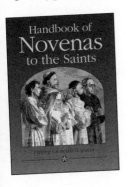

ISBN: 978 1 86082 867 0

CTS Code: D733

Benedict XVI
THE FATHERS & WRITERS OF
THE FIRST MILLENNIUM
The Spiritual Masters

The ten catecheses in this richly illustrated volume take us back to the historical period immediately following the first Fathers of the Church. Each of the Spiritual Masters described by Pope Benedict left their own mark on the Church's culture and spirituality and helped in her growth.

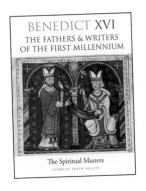

BENEDICT XVI
THE FATHERS & WRITERS
OF THE FIRST MILLENNIUM

The Spiritual Masters
CATHOLIC TRUTH SOCIETY

ISBN: 978 1 86082 772 8

CTS Code: B739

Benedict XVI
THE MEDIEVAL
FATHERS & WRITERS
The Spiritual Masters

Through his series of catecheses on the life and works of
great witnesses to the faith, Pope Benedict XVI helps us to
understand "what it means to be a Christian today." These
portraits of the distinguished figures of the medieval
Church are not just biographical sketches but also provide
the ecclesial backdrop against which they lived out their
'yes' to Christ. Through the words of the Holy Father, these
great Saints and teachers of the faith come alive and call us
to reawaken and deepen our own faith.

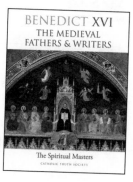

BENEDICT XVI
THE MEDIEVAL
FATHERS & WRITERS

The Spiritual Masters
CATHOLIC TRUTH SOCIETY

ISBN: 978 1 86082 723 5

CTS Code: B740